*I dedicate this book to the two most important
partnerships in my life: my husband, Don Marquis,
and my colleague, Carol Huston*

Bessie L. Marquis

*I dedicate this book to Tom,
my wonderful husband of 35 years.
I can't imagine my life without you.*

Carol J. Huston

Preface

We are excited about bringing our readers this new textbook, *Leadership and Management Tools for the New Nurse*. As those who are familiar with our textbook *Leadership Roles and Management Functions* know, we designed that book primarily for baccalaureate and graduate nursing students. In this new endeavor, we adapted that text, now in its 7th edition, to create a book more appropriate for use with the new nurse and in abbreviated leadership courses more commonly included in associate degree nursing programs.

While much of the content is similar in these two texts, adopters will find a new learning experience. Instead of Learning Exercises, we have developed case scenarios that are specific to the novice nurse. Virtually all of these case scenarios focus on the new staff nurse in the acute care setting or on the role transition that occurs between student nurse and new nurse. We have also added a *reflective thinking* section to improve critical thinking in the learner.

While this book provides an overview of leadership and management theory, it is not meant to be as broadly inclusive as its predecessor. For instance, none of the case scenarios deal with a level of management beyond the charge nurse level. Additionally, some of the topics covered in *Leadership Roles and Management Functions* were deleted in this book and some material has been presented differently. We have also attempted to focus on the staff nurse and team leader roles providing novice nurses with the skills and information necessary to become successful in their new roles.

It is our hope that this new textbook will meet a need in nursing education and will assist new graduate nurses in developing their leadership and management skills.

Contents

Unit 1

THE ESSENTIAL TOOLS OF EFFECTIVE LEADERSHIP AND MANAGEMENT

Chapter 1

UNDERSTANDING THE CHARACTERISTICS OF LEADERSHIP AND MANAGEMENT

Learning Objectives

The learner will be able to:

1. Identify various roles of a leader.
2. Identify the management process.
3. Describe the evolution of management and leadership development.
4. Identify common leadership styles.
5. Describe interactional and transformational leadership.
6. Describe types of followers found in organizations.
7. Identify characteristics of a servant leader.
8. Define emotional intelligence.
9. Discuss the cultural bridging role in leadership.

nurses work in a variety of health care organizations, interact with many levels of health care professionals, supervise the work of others, and organize their own workload. Thus, every nurse, even novice nurses, manage and lead to some degree. All nurses, then, must have some understanding of current and past development of management and leadership concepts.

Throughout history, organizations have adapted and changed in response to social and scientific advances. This adaptation is apparent when examining how leadership and management have interacted with one another from the 1900s to the present.

Management science developed prior to organizations becoming aware that good leadership was at least an equally, if not a more, important component of a progressive organization. Presently, most researchers agree that there is a symbiotic relationship between management and leadership. For example, a good manager must possess good leadership skills and an effective leader must be able to perform some of the duties of a good manager.

This chapter examines differences and similarities between leadership and management, the historical development of management science, and emerging views of leadership development.

The Management and Leadership Relationship

Leadership and management, and the relationship between them, continue to be debated. Most theorists agree that they are intertwined and, although different, are equally necessary. Leadership without management results in chaos and managers who cannot lead will be unable to empower others. McCarthy & Fitzpatrick (2009) maintain that there continues to be much ambiguity in the identification of management and leadership competences. Therefore, delineating what managers and leaders are may be helpful.

Management may be defined as successfully controlling something, such as an organization's financial or human resources. It is often defined as directing and supervising others. Just as there are many definitions and functions of management, there are also many levels of managers. Even a team leader with one person on his or her team is a manager. Marquis & Huston (2012) identify seven components of most management positions, which are listed in Table 1.1.

The study of *leadership* in organizations developed much later than management theory but presently commands the attention of researchers since it has become clear that good leadership has a profound effect upon organizational effectiveness. Leaders carry out many roles. Among other roles, they are teachers, visionaries, decision makers, and mentors. Indeed, leadership is often defined by the roles leaders perform. For example, Ward (2009) states that the leader is not only inspirational but is also the director of the action, and leaders have a combination of skills and personality traits that make others want to follow them.

In comparing what leaders and managers do, it becomes obvious that, as a new nurse, one may have an opportunity to be a leader even though he or she may not have an assigned management role. Remember that leadership is an important part of good management, but the reverse is not necessarily true as one does not have to have an assigned management position to be a leader. However, the authors will usually refer to leaders and managers by the use of the